Hear the Good News

Services for Maundy Thursday,
Good Friday, and Easter Sunrise

HOWARD ESHBAUGH

Lima, Ohio
C.S.S. Publishing Company

I0190239

HEAR THE GOOD NEWS

Copyright © 1984 by
The C.S.S. Publishing Company, Inc.
Lima, Ohio

All rights reserved. No portion of this book may be reproduced or utilized in any form or by any means, electronic or mechanical including photocopying, without permission in writing from the publisher. Inquiries should be addressed to: The C.S.S. Publishing Company, Inc., 628 South Main Street, Lima, Ohio 45804.

Permission is given to duplicate those parts of the service needed for congregational participation.

0805/ISBN 0-89536-656-8   PRINTED IN U.S.A.

TABLE OF CONTENTS

INTRODUCTION

These services for Maundy Thursday, Good Friday, and Easter Sunrise Service feature dramatic readings of the narratives as found in the synoptic Gospels (Matthew, Mark, and Luke). In addition to these dramatic readings of the action of the first Holy Week, other portions of Scripture are used as antiphonal hymns and liturgies.

These services are prepared with the understanding that God's Word, Scripture, is dynamic and lively. However, this cutting edge is often lost by some who read the Word as if it were static. Those who lead these worship services must prepare and practice so that they might read with feeling, showing the highs and lows of the text.

Before use of Scripture, the worship leader should give a brief explanation of the Scripture passage. An alternative of this presentation would be to place notes in the bulletin.

THE CALL TO WORSHIP

The call to worship is Psalm 117 with Christian responses. Psalm 117 is one of the Hallel Psalms (Psalms 113 to 118) that were used in praise of God during Passover worship.

ANTIPHONAL HYMNS

The form of an antiphonal hymn is quite simple. The congregation merely repeats what the leader has "lined out." If the leader sings, they sing. If the leader speaks softly, they speak softly. The words in capital letters are to be sung, the words in upper and lower case are to be spoken. The singing should be somewhat chantlike in form. The leader should mark the words to be sung with notations of the pitch desired. They may be done by placing dots above the words noting high or low notes over each syllable to be sung.

If no one in your group is able to lead the singing,

these hymns may be used in speaking all the phrases. Some instructions are given concerning tempo and dynamics.

The antiphonal hymns at the beginning of worship are Psalms of praise (Maundy Thursday, Psalm 100; Good Friday, Psalm 85:1-7; and Easter Sunrise, Psalm 98:1-3). These boldly proclaim the mighty deeds of God. The second hymn of Maundy Thursday, Exodus 5:1b-3, tells of the result of the Passover, God's people escape from Egypt. The final antiphonal hymns (Maundy Thursday, 2 Timothy 2:11, 13; Good Friday, 1 Timothy 1:15, 17; and Easter Sunrise, 1 Corinthians 15:3-6) are early creeds that tell of Jesus Christ.

THE LITANY

The body of the litany is Philippians 2:5-11 with the response from 2 Corinthians 8:6. Philippians 2:5-11 is an early Christian hymn. It has been described as the "gospel in a nutshell." It tells of the incarnation, ministry, death, and resurrection of Jesus Christ. On Maundy Thursday, only the parts telling of his incarnation and service are used. On Good Friday the portion telling of his death is added. For the Easter Sunrise service, the entire passage is used. The response tells of Jesus' humility and ministry.

DRAMATIC SCRIPTURE READINGS

Some churches may choose to use the same reader for smaller parts. This may be done if the readings are not too close together.

For a less choppy presentation, some may opt to delete phrases by the narrator as "they said" (Matthew 27:4b).

Those who read should mark the text to show what words are to be accented and what emotion is to be utilized in the reading. All must read slowly. This is imperative. ALL MUST READ SLOWLY.

The reader of Psalms 42, 43, and 22 in the Good Friday service must prepare very meticulously for these readings. It is essential that the reader be able to portray the pathos of these Psalms. The Psalms should be read from the *Revised Standard Version* or *The Jerusalem Bible*. If *The Jerusalem Bible* is used, substitute "Lord" or "the Lord" for Yahweh.

Maundy Thursday

Call to Worship

Leader: Praise the Lord, all nations.
People: Christ died for our sins.
Leader: Extol him, all peoples.
People: Christ was buried but was raised from the dead.
Leader: For great is his steadfast love toward us.
People: In love God gave his Son.
Leader: The faithfulness of the Lord endures forever.
People: God's faithfulness has been shown to us in Christ.
All: Praise the Lord.

Prayer (unison)

Father God, we come together on this night to remember Jesus' celebration of the passover with his disciples. Through your written word and through your Spirit enable us to experience what happened on that night and what it means to us. Amen.

Hymn

Psalm 100 is to be sung antiphonally (see instructions in the introduction). If desired, a hymn suitable for Maundy Thursday may be substituted.

MAKE A JOYFUL NOISE
A NOISE TO THE LORD
A noise to the Lord
A joyful noise to the Lord.
SERVE THE LORD WITH GLADNESS
serve with gladness
with gladness.
COME INTO HIS PRESENCE
HIS PRESENCE WITH SINGING
his presence
with singing.
KNOW THAT THE LORD IS GOD
The Lord is God.
IT IS HE THAT MADE US
and we are his
are his.
WE ARE HIS PEOPLE
his people
and the sheep of his pasture.
ENTER HIS GATES
ENTER WITH THANKSGIVING
and his courts with praise
enter with thanksgiving
enter with praise
praise and thanksgiving.
GIVE THANKS TO HIM
BLESS HIS NAME
bless and thank.
FOR THE LORD IS GOOD
THE LORD IS GOOD
his steadfast love endures forever.
His steadfast love
and his faithfulness to all generations
his faithfulness.
MAKE A JOYFUL NOISE.
serve the Lord
come, enter

give thanks, bless
THE LORD IS GOD.
The Lord is good.
AMEN

Litany: Philippians 2:5-7

Let the worship leader explain this passage of Scripture.

Philippians 2:5-11 is an early Christian hymn. It has been described as the "gospel in a nutshell." It tells of the incarnation, ministry, death, and resurrection of Jesus Christ. This evening, only the parts telling of his incarnation and service are used. The other verses will be added on Good Friday and Easter Sunrise service. The response in the litany is 2 Corinthians 8:9 which tells of the humility and service of Jesus Christ.

Leader:	Have this mind among yourselves, which you have in Christ Jesus.
People:	**For you know the grace of our Lord Jesus Christ, that though he was rich, yet for your sake he became poor, so that by his poverty you might become rich.**
Leader:	Who though he was in the form of God did not count equality with God a thing to be grasped.
People:	**For you know the grace of our Lord Jesus Christ, that though he was rich, yet for your sake he became poor, so that by his poverty you might become rich.**
Leader:	But he emptied himself, taking the form of a servant, being born in the likeness of men.
People:	**For you know the grace of our Lord Jesus Christ, that though he was rich,**

	yet for your sake he became poor, so that by his poverty you might become rich.
Leader:	And being found in human form he humbled himself.
People:	**For you know the grace of our Lord Jesus Christ, that though he was rich, yet for your sake he became poor, so that by his poverty you might become rich.**
All:	**Amen.**

Scripture: Mark 14:12a-22a

The readers necessary for this lesson are a narrator, Jesus, and disciple. (See instructions.)

Narrator:	And on the first day of Unleavened Bread, when they sacrificed the passover lamb, his disciples said to him, (14:12a)
Disciple:	"Where will you have us go and prepare for you to eat the passover?" (14:12b)
Narrator:	And he sent two of his disciples, and said to them, (14:13a)
Jesus:	"Go into the city, and a man carrying a jar of water will meet you; follow him, and wherever he enters say to the householder, 'The Teacher says, Where is my guest room, where I am to eat the passover with my disciples?' And he will show you a large upper room furnished and ready; there prepare for us." (14:13b-15)
Narrator:	And the disciples set out and went to the

city, and found it as he had told them; and they prepared the passover. And when it was evening, he came with the twelve. And as they were at table eating, Jesus said, (14:16-18a)

Jesus: "Truly, I say to you, one of you will betray me, one who is eating with me." (14:18b)

Narrator: They began to be sorrowful, and to say to him one after another, (14:19a)

Disciple: "Is it I?" (14:19a)

Narrator: He said to them, (14:20a)

Jesus: "It is one of the twelve, one who is dipping bread in the same dish with me. For the Son of man goes, as it is written of him, but woe to that man by whom the Son of man is betrayed! It would have been better for that man if he had not been born." (14:20b-21)

Narrator: And as they were eating, he took bread, and blessed, and broke it, and gave it to them, and said, (14:22a)

Jesus: "Take; this is my body." (14:22b)

Narrator: And he took a cup, and when he had given thanks, he gave it to them, and they all drank of it. And he said to them, (14:23-24a)

Jesus: "This is my blood of the covenant, which is poured out for many. Truly, I say to you, I shall not drink again of the fruit of the vine

until that day when I drink it new in the king-
dom of God." (14:24b-25)

The Lord's Supper

*The Lord's Supper will be celebrated in simplicity and in a
manner that the congregation can follow. It is suggested
that the words from Mark's Gospel be used as the rubrics
of celebration.*

Hymn

*Exodus 15:1b-3 is the oldest hymn of the Bible. It tells of
Israel's escape from Egypt by the power of God. This
deliverance followed the first passover. It is to be sung
antiphonally. (See instructions in the introduction.) If
desired, a hymn suitable for Maundy Thursday may be
substituted.*

I WILL SING TO THE LORD
SING TO THE LORD
for he has triumphed gloriously
triumphed gloriously.
The horse and its rider he has thrown
thrown them into the sea.
THE LORD IS MY STRENGTH
THE LORD IS MY SONG
strength and song.
HE HAS BECOME MY SALVATION
strength, song, salvation.
THIS IS MY GOD.
I WILL PRAISE HIM.
my father's God
I WILL EXALT HIM.
The Lord is a man of war.
THE LORD IS HIS NAME.
SING TO THE LORD

my strength, song, and salvation.
Amen.

Scripture: Mark 14:26-72

The readers necessary for this lesson are a narrator, Jesus, Peter, Judas, Accuser, High Priest, maid, bystander. (See instructions.)

Narrator: And when they had sung a hymn, they went out to the Mount of Olives. (14:26)

Narrator: And Jesus said to them, (14:27a)

Jesus: "You will all fall away; for it is written, 'I will strike the shepherd, and the sheep will be scattered.' But after I am raised up, I will go before you to Galilee." (14:27b-28)

Narrator: Peter said to him, (14:29a)

Peter: "Even though they all fall away, I will not." (14:29b)

Narrator: And Jesus said to him, (14:30a)

Jesus: "Truly, I say to you, this very night, before the cock crows twice, you will deny me three times." (14:30b)

Narrator: But he said vehemently, (14:31a)

Peter: "If I must die with you, I will not deny you." (14:31b)

Narrator: And they all said the same. (14:31c)

Narrator:	And they went to a place which was called Gethsemane; and he said to his disciples, (14:32a)
Jesus:	"Sit here, while I pray." (14:32b)
Narrator:	And he took with him Peter and James and John, and began to be greatly distressed and troubled. And he said to them, (14:33-34a)
Jesus:	My soul is very sorrowful, even to death; remain here, and watch." (14:34b)
Narrator:	And going a little farther, he fell on the ground and prayed that if it were possible, the hour might pass from him. And he said, (14:35-36a)
Jesus:	"Abba, Father, all things are possible to thee: remove this cup from me; yet not what I will, but what thou wilt." (14:36b)
Narrator:	And he came and found them sleeping, and he said to Peter, (14:37a)
Jesus:	"Simon, are you alseep? Could you not watch one hour? Watch and pray that you may not enter into temptation; the spirit indeed is willing, but the flesh is weak." (14:37b-38)
Narrator:	And again he went away and prayed, saying the same words. And again he came and found them sleeping, for their eyes were very heavy; and they did not know what to answer him. And he came the third

time, and said to them, (14:39-41a)

Jesus: "Are you still sleeping and taking your rest? It is enough; the hour has come; the Son of man is betrayed into the hands of sinners. Rise, let us be going; see, my betrayer is at hand." (14:41b-42)

Narrator: And immediately, while he was still speaking, Judas came, one of the twelve, and with him a crowd with swords and clubs, from the chief priests and the scribes and the elders. Now the betrayer had given them a sign, saying, (14:43-44a)

Judas: "The one I shall kiss is the man; seize him and lead him away safely." (14:44b)

Narrator: And when he came, he went up to him at once, and said, (14:45a)

Judas: "Master." (14:45b)

Narrator: And he kissed him. And they laid hands on him and seized him. But one of those who stood by drew his sword and struck the slave of the high priest and cut off his ear. And Jesus said to them, (14:45c-48a)

Jesus: "Have you come out as against a robber, with swords and clubs to capture me? Day after day I was with you in the temple teaching, and you did not seize me. But let the scriptures be fulfilled." (14:48b-49)

Narrator: And a young man followed him with nothing but a linen cloth about his body; and they seized him, but he left the linen cloth and ran away naked. And they led Jesus to the high priest; and all the high priests and the elders and the scribes were assembled. And Peter had followed him at a distance, right into the courtyard of the high priest; and he was sitting with the guards, and warming himself at the fire. Now the chief priests and the whole council sought testimony against Jesus, to put him to death; but they found none. For many bore false witness against him, and their witnesses did not agree. And some stood up and bore false witness against him, saying, (14:51-57)

Accuser: "We heard him say, 'I will destroy this temple that is made with hands, and in three days I will build another, not made with hands.'" (14:58)

Narrator: Yet not even so did their testimony agree. And the high priest stood up in the midst, and asked Jesus, (14:59-60a)

High Priest: "Have you no answer to make? What is it that these men testify against you?" (14:60b)

Narrator: But he was silent and made no answer. Again the high priest asked him, (14:61a)

High Priest: "Are you the Christ, the Son of the Blessed?" (14:61b)

Narrator: And Jesus said, (14:62a)

Jesus: "I am; and you will see the Son of man sitting at the right hand of Power, and coming with the clouds of heaven." (14:62b)

Narrator: And the high priest tore his mantle, and said, (14:63a)

High Priest: "Why do we still need witnesses? You have heard his blasphemy. What is your decision?" (14:63b)

Narrator: And they all condemned him as deserving death. And some began to spit on him, and to cover his face, and to strike him, saying to him, (14:64c)

Accuser: "Prophesy!" (14:65b)

Narrator: And the guards received him with blows. (14:65c)

Narrator: And as Peter was below in the courtyard, one of the maids of the high priest came, and seeing Peter warming himself, she looked at him and said, (14:66-67a)

Maid: "You also were with the Nazarene, Jesus." (14:67b)

Narrator: But he denied it, saying, (14:68a)

Peter: "I neither know nor understand what you mean." (14:68b)

Narrator: And he went out into the gateway. And the maid saw him, and began to say to bystanders, (14:68c-69a)

Maid: "This man is one of them." (14:69b)

Narrator:	But again he denied it. And after a little while again the bystanders said to Peter, (14:70a)
Bystander:	"Certainly you are one of them; for you are a Galilean." (14:70b)
Narrator:	But he began to invoke a curse on himself and to swear, (14:71a)
Peter:	"I do not know this man of whom you speak." (14:71b)
Narrator:	And immediately the cock crowed a second time. And Peter remembered how Jesus had said to him, "Before the cock crows twice, you will deny me three times." And he broke down and wept. (14:72)

Prayer (unison)

Forgive us, O God, for the times in our lives when we too have been less than faithful to Jesus Christ. Hear us now as we individually confess these deeds: _____
Forgive, O God, and through the Spirit equip us to be more faithful to Christ. Amen.

Hymn

2 Timothy 2:8, 11-13 is an early church creed. It is to be sung antiphonally. If desired, a hymn suitable for Maundy Thursday may be substituted.

REMEMBER JESUS CHRIST
remember Jesus Christ
RISEN FROM THE DEAD
DESCENDED FROM DAVID

PREACHED BY PAUL AS GOOD NEWS
THE GOOD NEWS.
remember Jesus Christ
descended, risen, proclaimed.
THE SAYING IS SURE
sure, certain, dependable.
IF WE DIE WITH HIM
WE ALSO SHALL LIVE WITH HIM
die and live.
IF WE ENDURE
WE ALSO SHALL REIGN WITH HIM
endure and reign.
IF WE DENY HIM
HE ALSO WILL DENY US
deny and be denied.
IF WE ARE FAITHLESS
HE REMAINS FAITHFUL.
He is faithful.
REMEMBER JESUS CHRIST
The faithful one.
Amen.

Benediction

Good Friday

Call to Worship

Leader: Praise the Lord, all nations.
People: **Christ died for our sins.**
Leader: Extol him, all peoples.
People: **Christ was buried but was raised from the dead.**
Leader: For great is his steadfast love toward us.
People: **In love God gave his Son.**
Leader: The faithfulness of the Lord endures forever.
People: **God's faithfulness has been shown to us in Christ.**
All: **Praise the Lord,**

Prayer (unison)

Father God, we come together on this day (night) to remember the crucifixion of Jesus Christ. Through your written word and through your Spirit enable us to experience what happened on that first Good Friday and what it means to us. Amen.

Hymn

Psalm 95:1-7 is to be sung antiphonally. (See instructions.) If desired, a hymn suitable for Good Friday may be substituted.

16

Come
LET US SING TO THE LORD
SING TO THE LORD
let us make a joyful noise
joyful noise *(almost a shout)*
joyful noise to the rock of our salvation
the rock of our salvation. *(slowly and deliberately)*
COME INTO GOD'S PRESENCE
WITH THANKSGIVING.
Make a joyful noise to him
joyful noise with SONGS OF PRAISE.
for the Lord is a great God
a great God
and a great king above all gods
A GREAT GOD AND KING.
In his hands are the depths of the earth.
The heights of the mountains are God's.
The sea is God's.
He made it.
His hands formed the dry land.
Depths
heights
sea
land
ARE ALL GOD'S.
COME LET US WORSHIP.
COME LET US BOW DOWN.
Let us kneel before the Lord
the Lord our maker.
THE LORD IS OUR GOD.
We are the people of God's pasture.
We are the sheep of God's hand.
THE LORD IS OUR GOD.

Litany: Philippians 2:5-8)

Today (This evening) only the parts telling of his incar-

nation, service, and death are used. The response in the litany is 2 Corinthians 8:9 which tells of the humility and service of Jesus Christ. On Maundy Thursday parts of this litany telling of his incarnation and service were used. Today (Tonight) the passage of his death is added. The complete passage will be used on Easter.

Leader: Have this mind among yourselves, which you have in Christ Jesus.

People: For you know the grace of our Lord Jesus Christ, that though he was rich, yet for your sake he became poor, so that by his poverty you might become rich.

Leader: Who though he was in the form of God did not count equality with God a thing to be grasped.

People: For you know the grace of our Lord Jesus Christ, that though he was rich, yet for your sake he became poor, so that by his poverty you might become rich.

Leader: But he emptied himself, taking the form of a servant, being born in the likeness of men.

People: For you know the grace of our Lord Jesus Christ, that though he was rich, yet for your sake he became poor, so that by his poverty you might become rich.

Leader: And being found in human form, he humbled himself and became obedient unto death, even death on a cross.

People: For you know the grace of our Lord Jesus Christ, that though he was rich, yet for your sake he became poor, so that by his poverty you might become

18

	rich.
All:	**Amen.**

Scripture: Matthew 27:1-54

The scriptural narrative, Matthew 27:1-54, that tells of the trial and crucifixion of Jesus will be interspersed with readings of some Psalms. This passion narrative includes illusions (27:35, 39) and quotation (27:45) of portions of Psalm 22. This worship service suggests that other Psalms may have come to the mind of Jesus in his trial and crucifixion. Hence, some Psalms are read in order to sense what Jesus may have sensed during his agony.

The Psalms must be read slowly and with feeling. The Psalms should be read from either the Revised Standard Version *. . . or* The Jerusalem Bible. *If* The Jerusalem Bible *is used, substitute "Lord" or "the Lord" for Yahweh.*

The readers needed for this passage are Narrator, Judas, a Chief Priest, Pilate, Jesus, Pilate's wife, a crowd (all voices except Jesus and Pilate), a soldier. The Psalms are to be read by the reader Jesus.

Narrator:	When morning came, all the chief priests and the elders of the people took counsel against Jesus to put him to death; and they bound him and led him away and delivered him to Pilate the governor. (27:1-2)
Narrator:	When Judas, his betrayer, saw that he was condemned, he repented and brought back the thirty pieces of silver to the chief priests and the elders, saying, (27:3)
Judas:	"I have sinned in betraying innocent blood." (27:4)

Narrator: They said, (27:4)

Priest: "What is that to us? See to it yourself."
             (27:4)

Narrator: And throwing down the pieces of silver in
             the temple, he departed; and went and
             hanged himself. (27:5)

Narrator: But the chief priests, taking the pieces of
             silver, said, (27:6)

Priest: "It is not lawful to put them into the trea-
             sury, since they are blood money." (27:6)

Narrator: So they took counsel, and bought with them
             the potter's field, to bury strangers in. There-
             fore that field has been called the Field of
             Blood to this day. Then was fulfilled what
             had been spoken by the prophet Jeremiah,
             saying,
                 "And they took the thirty pieces of sil-
             ver, the price of him on whom a price had
             been set by some of the sons of Israel, and
             they gave them for the potter's field, as the
             Lord directed me." (27:7-10)

Narrator: Now Jesus stood before the governor; and
             the governor asked him, (27:11)

Pilate: "Are you the King of the Jews?" (27:11)

Narrator: Jesus said to him, (27:11)

Jesus: "You have said so." (27:11)

Narrator: But when he was accused by the chief

priests and elders, he made no answer. Then Pilate said to him, (27:12-13)

Pilate: "Do you not hear how many things they testify against you?" (27:13)

Narrator: But he gave him no answer, not even to a single charge; so that the governor wondered greatly. (27:14)

Psalm 42 read by Jesus.

Narrator: Now at the feast the governor was accustomed to release for the crowd any one prisoner whom they wanted. And they had then a notorious prisoner, called Barabbas. So when they had gathered, Pilate said to them, (27:15-16)

Pilate: "Whom do you want me to release for you, Barabbas or Jesus who is called Christ?" (27:17)

Narrator: For he knew that it was out of envy that they had delivered him up. Besides, while he was sitting on the judgment seat, his wife sent word to him, (27:18-19)

Wife: "Have nothing to do with that righteous man, for I have suffered much over him today in a dream." (27:19)

Narrator: Now the chief priests and the elders persuaded the people to ask for Barabbas and destroy Jesus. The governor again said to them, (27:20)

Pilate: "Which of the two do you want me to release for you?" (27:21)

Narrator: And they said, (27:21)

Crowd: "Barabbas." (27:21)

Narrator: Pilate said to them, (27:22)

Pilate: "Then what shall I do with Jesus who is called Christ?" (27:22)

Narrator: They all said, (27:23)

Crowd: "Let him be crucified." (27:23)

Narrator: And he said, (27:23)

Pilate: "Why, what evil has he done?" (27:23)

Narrator: But they shouted all the more, (27:23)

Crowd: "Let him be crucified." (27:23)

Narrator: So when Pilate saw that he was gaining nothing, but rather that a riot was beginning, he took water and washed his hands before the crowd saying, (27:24)

Pilate: "I am innocent of this man's blood; see to it yourselves." (27:24)

Narrator: And all the people answered, (27:25)

Crowd: "His blood be on us and on our children!" (27:25)

Narrator: Then he released for them Barabbas, and having scourged Jesus, delivered him to be crucified. (27:26)

Psalm 43 read by Jesus.

Narrator: Then the soldiers of the governor took Jesus into the praetorium, and they gathered the whole battalion before him. And they stripped him and put a scarlet robe upon him, and plating a crown of the thorns, they put it on his head, and put a reed in his right hand. And kneeling before him, they mocked him, saying, (27:27-29)

Soldiers: "Hail, King of the Jews!" (27:29)

Narrator: And they spat upon him, and took the reed and struck him on the head. And when they had mocked him, they stripped him of the robe, and put his own clothes on him, and led him away to crucify him. (27:30-31)

Narrator: As they were marching out, they came upon a man of Cyrene, Simon by name; this man they compelled to carry his cross. And when they came to a place called Golgotha, which means the place of a skull, they offered him wine to drink, mingled with gall; but when he tasted it, he would not drink it. And when they had crucified him, they divided his garments among them by casting lots; then they sat down and kept watch over him there. And over his head, they put the charge against him, which read, "This is Jesus the King of the Jews." Then two robbers were crucified with him, one on the right and one on the left. And those who passed by derided him, wagging their heads and saying, (27:32-39)

Passersby: "You who would destroy the temple and build it in three days, save yourself! If you are the Son of God, come down from the cross." (27:40)

Narrator: So also the chief priests, with the scribes and elders, mocked him, saying, (27:41)

Chief Priests: "He saved others; he cannot save himself. He is the King of Israel; let him come down now from the cross, and we will believe in him. He trusts in God; let God deliver him now, if he desires him; for he said, 'I am the Son of God.'" (27:42-43)

Narrator: And the robbers who were crucified with him also reviled him in the same way. (27:44)

Narrator: Now from the sixth hour there was darkness over all the land until the ninth hour. And about the ninth hour Jesus cried with a loud voice, (27:45)

Jesus: "Eli, Eli, lama sabachthani?" "My God, my God, why hast thou forsaken me?"

Narrator: And some of the bystanders hearing it said, (27:47)

Crowd: "This man is calling Elijah." (27:47)

Narrator: And one of them at once ran and took a

sponge, filled it with vinegar, and put it on a reed, and gave it to him to drink. But the others said, (27:48-49)

Crowd: "Wait, let us see whether Elijah will come to save him." (27:49)

Narrator: And Jesus cried again with a loud voice and yielded up his spirit. (27:50)

Narrator: And behold, the curtain of the temple was torn in two, from top to bottom; and the earth shook, and the rocks were split; the tombs also were opened, and many bodies of the saints who had fallen asleep were raised, and coming out of the tombs after his resurrection they went into the holy city and appeared to many. When the centurion and those who were with him, keeping watch over Jesus, saw the earthquake and what took place, they were filled with awe, and said, (27:51-54)

Centurion: "Truly this was the son of God!" (27:54)

Psalm 22

Let the worship leader explain.

Psalm 22 is both a cry of anguish and a Psalm of praise. The cry of Jesus, "My God, my God, why have you forsaken me?" is not the last word. Good Friday only becomes "good" through the victory of Easter. Psalm 22 is read as the conclusion of this Good Friday service to show the anguish of Jesus on the cross but also to affirm his triumph on the resurrection.

Psalm 22 read by Jesus.

Prayer

As we stand at the foot of the cross, O God, we behold a love that goes beyond our understanding. Thank you, God, for Jesus Christ who died for our sins. Amen.

Hymn: 1 Timothy 1:15, 17

First Timothy 1:15, 17 is to be sung antiphonally. A hymn suitable for Good Friday may be substituted.

THE SAYING IS SURE
is sure.
THE SAYING IS WORTHY OF FULL ACCEPTANCE
worthy of full acceptance
SURE AND WORTHY
the saying is.
Christ Jesus came into the world
came into the world to save sinners.
CHRIST CAME TO SAVE SINNERS.
This is certain and sure
Christ came to save sinners.
TO THE KING OF AGES
immortal, invisible, the only God
BE HONOR
BE GLORY
to God be honor and glory
FOREVER AND EVER.
Amen.

Benediction

Easter Sunrise

Call to Worship

Leader: Praise the Lord, all nations.
People: Christ died for our sins.
Leader: Extol him, all peoples.
People: Christ was buried but was raised from the dead.
Leader: For great is his steadfast love toward us.
People: In love God gave his Son.
Leader: The faithfulness of the Lord endures forever.
People: God's faithfulness has been shown to us in Christ.
All: Praise the Lord.

Prayer (unison)

Father God, we come together on this morning to remember the resurrection of Jesus Christ. Through your written word and through your Spirit, enable us to experience what happened on that first Easter morning and what it means to us. Amen.

Hymn

Psalm 98:1-3 is to be sung antiphonally. If desired, a hymn suitable for Easter may be substituted.

SING
SING TO THE LORD
SING TO THE LORD A NEW SONG
a new song.
His right hand and his holy arm
have gotten him victory
VICTORY.
The Lord has made known his victory
VICTORY.
God has revealed this vindication
vindication.
VICTORY
God has remembered his steadfast love
steadfast love
steadfast love and faithfulness
to the house of Israel.
VICTORY
All the ends of the earth
have seen the victory
the victory of our God
VICTORY.
Amen.

Litany: Philippians 2:5-11

Let the worship leader explain the passage of Scripture.

Philippians 2:5-11 is an early Christian hymn. It has been described as the "gospel in a nutshell." It tells of the incarnation, ministry, death, and resurrection of Jesus Christ. In the services on Maundy Thursday and Good Friday, only portions of this passage were used. On this Easter day, the entire passage is used. The response is 2 Corinthians 8:9 which tells of the humility and service of Jesus Christ.

Leader: Have this mind among yourselves, which you have in Christ Jesus.

People: **For you know the grace of our Lord Jesus Christ, that though he was rich, yet for your sake he became poor, so that by his poverty you might become rich.**

Leader: Who though he was in the form of God did not count equality with God a thing to be grasped.

People: **For you know the grace of our Lord Jesus Christ, that though he was rich, yet for your sake he became poor, so that by his poverty you might become rich.**

Leader: But he emptied himself, taking the form of a servant, being born in the likeness of men.

People: **For you know the grace of our Lord Jesus Christ, that though he was rich, yet for your sake he became poor, so that by his poverty you might become rich.**

Leader: And being found in human form, he humbled himself and became obedient unto death, even death on a cross.

People: **For you know the grace of our Lord Jesus Christ, that though he was rich, yet for your sake he became poor, so that by his poverty you might become rich.**

Leader: Therefore God has highly exalted him and bestowed on him the name which is above every name.

People: **For you know the grace of our Lord Jesus Christ, that though he was rich, yet for your sake he became poor, so that by his poverty you might become rich.**

Leader: That at the name of Jesus every knee

should bow, in heaven and on earth and under the earth, and every tongue confess that Jesus Christ is Lord, to the glory of God the Father.

People: **For you know the grace of our Lord Jesus Christ, that though he was rich, yet for your sake he became poor, so that by his poverty you might become rich.**

All: **Amen.**

Scripture: Luke 24:1-52

The readers necessary for this reading are a narrator, angel, Jesus, Cleopas, and disciple. (See instructions.)

Narrator: But on the first day of the week, at early dawn, they went to the tomb, taking the spices which they had prepared. And they found the stone rolled away from the tomb, but when they went in, they did not find the body. While they were perplexed about this, behold, two men stood by them in dazzling apparel; and as they were frightened and bowed their faces to the ground, the men said to them, (24:1-5a)

Angel: "Why do you seek the living among the dead? Remember how he told you, while he was still in Galilee, that the Son of man must be delivered into the hands of sinful men, and be crucified, and on the third day rise." (24:5b-7)

Narrator: And they remembered his words, and returning from the tomb they told all this to the eleven and to all the rest. Now it was Mary

Magdalene and Joanna and Mary the mother of James and the other women with them who told this to the apostles, but these words seemed to them an idle talk, and they did not believe them. (24:8-12)

Narrator: That very day two of them were going to a village named Emmaus, about seven miles from Jerusalem, and talking with each other about all these things that had happened. While they were talking and discussing together, Jesus himself drew near and went with them. But their eyes were kept from recognizing him. And he said to them, (24:13-17a)

Jesus: "What is this conversation which you are holding with each other as you walk?" (24:17b)

Narrator: Then one of them, named Cleopas, answered him, (24:18)

Cleopas: "Are you the only visitor to Jerusalem who does not know the things that have happened there in these days?" (24:18b)

Narrator: And he said to them, (24:19a)

Jesus: "What things?" (24:19b)

Narrator: And they said to him, (24:19c)

Cleopas: "Concerning Jesus of Nazareth, who was a prophet mighty in deed and word before God and all the people, and how our chief priests and rulers delivered him up to be condemned to death and crucified him. But we had hoped that he was the one to redeem Israel. Yes, and besides all this, it is now the third day since this happened. Moreover, some women of our company amazed us, they were at the tomb early in the morning and did not find his body, and they came back saying that they had even seen a vision of angels, who said that he was alive. Some of those who were with us went to the tomb, and found it just as the women had said; but him they did not see." (24:19d-24)

Narrator: And he said to them, (24:25a)

Jesus: "O foolish men, and slow of heart to believe all that the prophets have spoken! Was it not necessary that the Christ should suffer these things and enter into his glory?" (24:25b-26)

Narrator: And beginning with Moses and all the prophets, he interpreted to them in all the scriptures the things concerning himself. (24:27)

Narrator: So they drew near to the village to which they were going; and he made as though he would go further, but they constrained him, saying, (24:28-29a)

Cleopas: "Stay with us, for it is toward evening and the day is now far spent." (24:29b)

Narrator: So he went in to stay with them. When he was at table with them, he took the bread and blessed, and broke it, and gave it to them. And their eyes were opened and they recognized him; and he vanished out of their sight. They said to each other, (24:29c-32a)

Cleopas: "Did not our hearts burn within us while he talked to us on the road, while he opened to us the Scriptures?" (24:32b)

Narrator: And they rose that same hour and returned to Jerusalem; and they found the eleven gathered together and those who were with them, who said, (24:33-34a)

Disciples: "The Lord has risen indeed, and has appeared to Simon!" (24:34b)

Narrator: Then they told what had happened on the road, and how he was known to them in the breaking of the bread. (24:35)

Narrator: As they were saying this, Jesus himself stood among them. But they were startled and frightened, and supposed that they saw a spirit. And he said to them, (24:36-38a)

Jesus: "Why are you troubled, and why do questionings rise in your hearts? See my hands and feet, that it is I myself; handle me, and see; for a spirit has not flesh and bones as you see that I have." (24:38b-40)

Narrator: And while they still disbelieved for joy, and wondered, he said to them, (24:41a)

Jesus: "Have you anything here to eat?" (24:41b)

Narrator: They gave him a piece of boiled fish, and he took it and ate before them. (24:42-43)

Narrator: Then he said to them, (24:44a)

Jesus: "These are my words which I spoke to you, while I was still with you, that everything written about me in the law of Moses and the prophets and the psalms must be fulfilled." (24:44b)

Narrator: Then he opened their minds to understand the scriptures, and said to them, (24:45-46a)

Jesus: "Thus it is written, that the Christ should suffer and on the third day rise from the dead, and that repentance and forgiveness of sins should be preached in his name to all nations, beginning from Jerusalem. You are witness to these things. And behold, I send the promise of my Father upon you; but stay in the city, until you are clothed with power from on high." (24:46b-49)

Narrator: Then he led them out as far as Bethany, and lifting up his hands, he blessed them. While he blessed them, he parted from them. And they returned to Jerusalem with great joy, and were continually in the temple blessing God. (24:50-52)

The Fish Meal

At this time, let each be given a fish-shaped cracker. (These are available in most grocery stores.) If a meal is to be served after the worship service, celebrate the Fish

Meal at the table.

Let the worship leader explain.

This fish cracker can symbolize many things:
1. Jesus called disciples who were fishers. They were told they would become fishers of men.
2. A fish was the first food eaten by the risen Christ.
3. In John's Gospel, the risen Jesus directs the disciples to a vast, symbolic (153) catch of fish. He later eats fish with them.
4. The fish is a symbol of Jesus Christ.
   The Greek word for fish is *ICHTHUS*.
   The I stands for *Jesus* — Jesus.
   The CH for *Christos* — Christ.
   The TH for *Theos* — God.
   The U for *Huios* — Son.
   The S for *Soter* — Savior.

This is the fish creed — Jesus Christ, God's Son, Savior. Let us affirm our faith by the creed and then eat the fish cracker. Jesus Christ, God's Son, Savior. Amen. *(Eat cracker.)*

Prayer

Father God, we thank you for the victory of the first Easter. As we remember this victory over sin and death, open our hearts that it may be part of our lives. Amen.

Hymn

First Corinthians 15:3-6 is to be sung antiphonally. (See instructions in the introduction.) If desired, a hymn suitable for Easter may be substituted.

Let the worship leader note.

First Corinthians 15:3-6 is a creedal affirmation about Jesus Christ. It is an announcement of the Good News.

HEAR THE GOOD NEWS
THE GOOD NEWS
The good news which you received
the good news in which you stand.
the good news by which your are saved.
CHRIST DIED FOR OUR SINS.
This is according to Scripture.
HE WAS BURIED
but on the third day he was raised.
This also is according to Scripture.
HE APPEARED TO PETER
to Peter.
HE APPEARED TO THE TWELVE
to Peter,
to the twelve.
HE APPEARED TO FIVE HUNDRED OTHERS
to Peter, to the twelve, to five hundred others.
THIS IS THE GOOD NEWS
THE GOOD NEWS.
Christ died for our sins.
Christ is raised from the dead.

Benediction

www.ingramcontent.com/pod-product-compliance
Lightning Source LLC
Chambersburg PA
CBHW060043040426
42331CB00032B/2246